The Word Wizard's Book of PRONOUNS

Robin Johnson

Crabtree
Publishing
Company
www.crabtreebooks.com

Word Wizard

Author
Robin Johnson

Publishing plan research and development
Reagan Miller

Editorial director
Kathy Middleton

Project coordinator
Kelly Spence

Editor
Anastasia Suen

Proofreader and indexer
Wendy Scavuzzo

Photo research
Robin Johnson, Katherine Berti

Design & prepress
Katherine Berti

Print coordinator
Katherine Berti

Photographs
Thinkstock: p 7 (bottom left)
All other images from Shutterstock

Library and Archives Canada Cataloguing in Publication

Johnson, Robin (Robin R.), author
    The word wizard's book of pronouns / Robin Johnson.

(Word wizard)
Includes index.
Issued in print and electronic formats.
ISBN 978-0-7787-1922-9 (bound).--ISBN 978-0-7787-1926-7 (pbk.).--
ISBN 978-1-4271-7794-0 (pdf).--ISBN 978-1-4271-7790-2 (html)

    1. English language--Pronoun--Juvenile literature. I. Title.

PE1261.J64 2015   j428.2   C2014-907802-1
                                      C2014-907803-X

Library of Congress Cataloging-in-Publication Data

Johnson, Robin (Robin R.)
 The Word Wizard's book of pronouns / Robin Johnson.
   pages cm. -- (Word Wizard)
 Includes index.
 ISBN 978-0-7787-1922-9 (reinforced library binding) --
 ISBN 978-0-7787-1926-7 (pbk.) -- ISBN 978-1-4271-7794-0 (electronic pdf) --
ISBN 978-1-4271-7790-2 (electronic html)
1. English language--Pronoun--Juvenile literature. 2. English language--
Parts of speech--Juvenile literature. 3. English language--Grammar--
Juvenile literature. 4. Language arts (Elementary) I. Title. II. Title: Book of
pronouns.

 PE1261.J66 2015
 425'.55--dc23
                                 2014045069

Crabtree Publishing Company

www.crabtreebooks.com   1-800-387-7650

Printed in Canada/022015/IH20141209

Published in Canada
Crabtree Publishing
616 Welland Ave.
St. Catharines, Ontario
L2M 5V6

Published in the United States
Crabtree Publishing
PMB 59051
350 Fifth Avenue, 59th Floor
New York, New York 10118

Published in the United Kingdom
Crabtree Publishing
Maritime House
Basin Road North, Hove
BN41 1WR

Published in Australia
Crabtree Publishing
3 Charles Street
Coburg North
VIC 3058

Contents

Magic words

Words can do anything! Some words make you disappear. Others chase clouds away. Some help you climb into bed. Others let you slide down rainbows. Some words open secret doors. Others open cookie jars! They are all magical.

You can do anything with words!

4

Magic jobs

Magic words do different jobs. Some words tell how things look. Others tell how they move. Some words are called **pronouns**. Pronouns help us name things. The Word Wizards want to learn more about pronouns. Will you help them become pronoun pros?

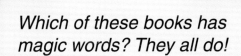

Which of these books has magic words? They all do!

What are pronouns?

Pronouns are words such as "I," "him," "all," "ours," and "myself." These words take the place of **nouns**. Nouns name people, animals, places, things, or ideas. The words "girl," "duck," and "home" are nouns. The words "toy" and "fun" are nouns. Your name is a noun, too!

There are different types of nouns. We use different types of pronouns to replace them.

Word Wizard in training

Help the Word Wizard spot the pronouns! Read the first **sentence** with each picture below. A sentence is a complete thought or idea. Find the noun in the sentence. Is it a person, animal, place, thing, or idea? Then read the second sentence. Which word replaced the noun? That is a pronoun!

Sentence #1: *Jeremy can jump high!*

Sentence #2: *He can jump high!*

Sentence #1: *The frog is hanging around.*

Sentence #2: *It is hanging around.*

Why do we need pronouns?

Pronouns help us **communicate**. To communicate means to share ideas and information. Pronouns let us tell our stories clearly with fewer words. They make our stories more interesting. Without pronouns, we would repeat the same nouns. Our stories would be long and boring.

These kids are communicating. They are sharing their feelings—and their popcorn!

Say it again

Look at the following sentences. "The girls made a big mess! The girls need to clean the mess up." The nouns "girls" and "mess" are repeated. How does the story sound? Now we will change some of the nouns to pronouns. "The girls made a big mess! They need to clean it up." The words "they" and "it" are pronouns. How do they make the story better?

He said, she said

We use **personal pronouns** to talk about **specific** people and things. Specific means a certain one. We use the pronoun "I" to talk about ourselves. It always has a capital letter. We say, "I like to play dress-up." The words "you," "he," "she," "we," "they," and "it" are other personal pronouns.

Do I make myself clear?

We use personal pronouns when it is clear who or what we are talking about. We say, "Josie cannot walk in those shoes. They are too big for her!" The pronoun "they" replaces the noun "shoes." The pronoun "her" replaces the noun "Josie." We can use those pronouns because the nouns give us information. They tell us who and what the sentence is about.

In general

We use **indefinite pronouns** to talk about general people or things. "Indefinite" means unknown or unclear. We say, "Does anyone want to play?" The word "anyone" is an indefinite pronoun. It does not refer to a specific person. We say, "I am bored. There is nothing to do!" The word "nothing" is an indefinite pronoun. It does not tell us about a specific thing.

This girl is taking care of somebody special.

This boy found something big to play with!

Word Wizard in training

Help the Word Wizard spy the pronouns! Some are shown in the box below. Point to the pronoun that completes each sentence best. Can you spy both of the answers?

all	something
any	none
both	nothing
each	several
everyone	some
few	neither
many	someone

I spy with my little eye _____ that is green.

I spy with my little eye _____ who is smart.

His and hers

Possessive pronouns tell us who **possesses** something. To possess means to have or to own. Look at the picture below. The boy has a cupcake. It is his. The word "his" is a possessive pronoun. It tells us the cupcake belongs to the boy. The girls cannot eat the cupcake. It is not theirs. "Theirs" is a possessive pronoun, too. The words "hers," "mine," "ours," and "yours" are other possessive pronouns.

Word Wizard
in training

Pick some pronouns for the Word Wizard! Point to the correct pronoun to complete each sentence. Then read the sentences aloud. You have an important job to do. It is all yours!

This girl got a new kitten! The kitten is [hers/his].

These pets are wearing party hats! The hats are [mine/theirs].

Me, myself, and I

The ballerina watches herself dance. The mirror reflects her moves.

Reflexive pronouns are words that act like mirrors. They **reflect** nouns and pronouns that come before them in sentences. They add more information to the sentences. We say, "I like to dance by myself." The word "myself" is a reflexive pronoun. It reflects the pronoun "I." The words "yourself," "itself," and "ourselves" are some other reflexive pronouns.

Word Wizard in training

Help the Word Wizard find the reflexive pronouns below. She cannot do it herself. She does not know that reflexive pronouns have the same endings. They all end with the **suffixes** "self" or "selves." Point to the reflexive pronoun in each sentence. Try to do it all by yourself!

Josh can tie his shoes himself.

The kids made a car for themselves!

Pronouns must agree

Pronouns must agree with the nouns they replace. We use different pronouns for boys and girls. We use "he," "him," "his," and "himself" for boys. We use "she," "her," "hers," and "herself" for girls. We do not say, "Henry helps make dinner. She is a good cook." Henry is a boy. We use a boy's pronoun to replace his name. We say, "He is a good cook."

he
himself

she
herself

Something about things

Things are neither boys nor girls. We use the pronouns "it" and "itself" to replace them. We do not say, "Amber bounces the basketball. She throws him." The basketball is not a boy! It is a thing. We say, "She throws it."

Singular and plural

We also use different pronouns for **singular** and **plural** nouns. Singular means only one. Plural means more than one. We use singular pronouns to replace singular nouns. We say, "The girl has an apple on her desk. She will eat it at recess." The nouns "girl" and "apple" are singular. We use the singular pronouns "she" and "it" to replace them.

Plural pronouns

We use plural pronouns to replace plural nouns. Plural pronouns are "they," "them," "theirs," and "themselves." We say, "The kids have apples on their heads! They will drop them and make applesauce." The nouns "kids" and "apples" are plural. We replace them with the plural pronouns "they" and "them."

Practice makes perfect

Now it is time to practice your pronouns! Help the Word Wizard match up words below. Use your finger to join a word from each box. Some of the words are nouns. Others are pronouns. Remember that they must agree. Pair them up and be a pronoun pro!

I	hers
you	them
the girls	mine
George	he
we	itself
Betty's	yourself
it	ours

Three cheers for you! You are a pronoun pro!

Learning more

Books

I and You and Don't Forget Who: What Is a Pronoun? (Words Are CATegorical) by Brian P. Cleary. First Avenue Editions, 2006.

If You Were a Pronoun (Word Fun) by Nancy Loewen. Picture Window Books, 2006.

Slam Dunk Pronouns (Grammar All-Stars) by Doris Fisher and D. L. Gibbs. Gareth Stevens Publishing, 2008.

Stand-In Pronouns Save the Scene! (Grammar's Slammin') by Pamela Hall. Magic Wagon, 2009.

Websites

Spot pronouns and pop balloons in this fun game.
www.softschools.com/language_arts/grammar/pronoun/balloon_game

Order words to make sentences in these two pronoun games.
http://learnenglishkids.britishcouncil.org/en/grammar-games/pronouns

Pick the pronouns in this speedy car rally game.
http://gotkidsgames.com/hom/easyPronounGame.html

Words to know

communicate (kuh-MYOO-ni-keyt) To share ideas and information

indefinite (in-DEF-uh-nit) Unknown or unclear

indefinite pronoun (in-DEF-uh-nit PROH-noun) A word that refers to a general person or thing

noun (noun) A word that names a person, animal, place, thing, or idea

personal pronoun (PUR-suh-nl PROH-noun) A word that refers to a specific person or thing

plural (PLOO R-uh l) More than one

possess (puh-ZES) To have or to own

possessive pronoun (puh-ZES-iv PROH-noun) A word that tells who has or owns something

pronoun (PROH-noun) A word that takes the place of a noun

reflect (ri-FLEKT) To act like a mirror and show something back

reflexive pronoun (ri-FLEK-siv PROH-noun) A word that reflects a noun or pronoun that comes before it

sentence (SEN-tns) A complete thought or idea

singular (SING-gyuh-ler) Only one

specific (spi-SIF-ik) A certain one

suffix (SUHF-iks) One or more letters added to the end of a word to change its meaning

Index